Giving up only becomes an option if you walk in life alone. In her book *Infinitely More*, my friend Kim Crabill reminds us that with Christ we are never alone, so giving up is not an option. Her writings dig into the scriptural truths that I've practiced on and off the field to accomplish more than I could ever imagine. No matter where you are in life, I believe this book will be just as powerful for you.

—Ray Lewis, NFL Hall of Famer
and *New York Times* best seller

My dear friend Kim Crabill has an extraordinary way of extracting great insights from Scripture that she then turns into practical and relevant advice for successful daily living. Whether you are young or old, male or female, you'll enjoy this devotional and keep coming back to it for years to come.

—Joe Battaglia, broadcaster, producer, and author of
The Politically Incorrect Jesus and *Unfriended*

Kim Crabill's *Infinitely More*, a forty-day devotional based on Ephesians 3:20, takes you on a journey of self-discovery while drawing you closer to Jesus. The devotional is Scripture-based and laced with personal stories and antidotes that bring clarity to the biblical message. I encourage you to read this book with a pen in hand so you can fill your journal pages as the Scriptures speak to you and your life is transformed by the message of hope.

—Dr. Barbara J. Parker, women's leadership specialist, Dallas Baptist Association

Your life can be infinitely more with Christ. Experience this journey with Kim Crabill and find freedom, courage, and spiritual abundance in Him.

—Suellen Roberts, founder and president of Christian Women in Media Association

Are you expecting great things from God? Are you looking for the potential and possibilities of what God wants to do in and through you? It's easy to allow disappointments to diminish our hope, but Kim Crabill brings us back to the promises in God's Word in this positive and inspiring devotional. *Infinitely More* will strengthen your heart and encourage your faith in the transforming work God is able to do in your life.

—Karol Ladd, best-selling author of *The Power of a Positive Woman*

Infinitely More is the devotional experience you've long awaited. Kim Crabill delivers spiritual insights from her own journey of honesty with God and self. This book is a must-have for the serious pursuer of godly character!

—Brenda Crouch, author, speaker, singer, and TV personality

40 DEVOTIONS

Infinitely More

THAN You CAN Ask OR Imagine

Kim Crabill

BroadStreet
P U B L I S H I N G

BroadStreet Publishing® Group, LLC
Savage, Minnesota, USA
BroadStreetPublishing.com

Infinitely More: THAN YOU COULD ASK OR IMAGINE

978-1-4245-5929-9 (faux leather)
978-1-4245-5930-5 (e-book)

Stock or custom editions of BroadStreet Publishing titles may be purchased in bulk for educational, business, ministry, fundraising, or sales promotional use. For information, please email info@broadstreetpublishing.com.

Cover and interior by Garborg Design at GarborgDesign.com

Printed in China

19 20 21 22 23 5 4 3 2 1

To my precious first granddaughter, Cohen Bailey.
May you always remember you are loved infinitely
more than you can imagine. Be assured that no
matter where life takes you, God's love goes with you.

Contents

Foreword 10

Introduction 13

DAY 1 Pearls 21

DAY 2 Could This Be the Day? 25

DAY 3 Stuck in the Right Place 28

DAY 4 Relationally Speaking 32

DAY 5 What a Masterpiece! 35

DAY 6 Called to Encourage 38

DAY 7 Need a Miracle? 42

DAY 8 You Are Here 46

DAY 9 Declaration of Hope 50

DAY 10 Heavenly Setups 53

DAY 11 Glorious Giggles 57

DAY 12 An Amazing Story 60

DAY 13 Unbelievable 63

DAY 14 Is Your God Able? 66

DAY 15 The Power of Thankfulness 70

DAY 16 To the Giver's Glory 73

DAY 17 Memories of Encouragement 76

DAY 18 A Promising Outcome 79

DAY 19 Who Knows? 82

DAY 20 We Need to Talk 86

DAY 21 Misery Requires Company 90

DAY 22 Pushing Buttons 93

DAY 23 Dream a Little Dream 97

DAY 24 Ready, Set, What? 100

DAY 25 What Will They Think? 104

DAY 26 An Invitation to Decline 107

DAY 27 Choose Life 110

DAY 28 Temporary Status 113

DAY 29 HALT 117

DAY 30 Bankable Truths 120

DAY 31 Seven Simple Words 123

DAY 32 Believe, Act, Receive 126

DAY 33 None Too Small 130

DAY 34 The Power to Care 134

DAY 35 Spelling Lesson 137

DAY 36 Calm Inside and Out 140

DAY 37 Believing the Best 144

DAY 38 Be Available 146

DAY 39 Messes Welcome 150

DAY 40 A Banquet Ahead 154

About the Author 159

Foreword

I first met Kim Crabill when I sat next to her at a friend's wedding. I never imagined I would develop such a precious, lifelong friendship with this elegant woman. Both our deep connection as women in ministry and her passion for seeing women's lives changed have been amazing blessings to me.

For someone who is so classy and sophisticated, you might never guess how much hardship she's had to overcome. The enemy tried to rob her of her future, but Kim has relied solely on Jesus. When she was weak, Christ made her strong! She definitely told the enemy, "Not today, satan! Not today!"

We tend to get exactly what we expect out of life and nothing more. Our meager expectations seem wholly pathetic compared to the vast wonders that the Creator of the universe has in mind for us. One thing is for sure: God always lives up to His promises! And His promises are so much more than we can ever imagine. In *Infinitely More*, Kim helps us truly understand how overwhelmingly infinite and unfathomable those promises really are!

Inspired by Ephesians 3:20, Kim immerses us in the depths of God's extravagant promises. With her confident voice, she breaks down the passage and presents it in a clever, understandable format so we never feel overwhelmed. *Infinitely More* is easy to study, put down, and pick up again, and you will never miss a beat. Anyone who's busy knows how invaluable that is.

Our lives are only limited by the boundaries of our own imaginations. Will we be able to release what's currently in our hands in order to receive infinitely more? We're ready, Kim, for an enlightening forty-day journey. Lead the way!

Nicole Crank, author, speaker,
senior co-pastor of Faith Church
(St. Louis & West Palm Beach)

Introduction

Now all glory to God, who is able,
through his mighty power at work within us,
to accomplish infinitely more
than we might ask or think.

EPHESIANS 3:20 NLT

Europe delighted us with its historical sights and wonders. I thought standing inside the Colosseum, looking down from the London Eye at Big Ben, or even standing before the Eiffel Tower would be the highlights of our trip. Yet our youngest son, Austin, was reserving his enthusiasm for the Matterhorn.

We arrived in Zermatt, Switzerland, to the disappointing sight of cloud-covered skies. One store owner assured us that, with a little luck, the winds might move the clouds to reveal the Alps. This is what Austin longed for.

Grabbing some hot chocolate, we sat and waited. Sure enough, the winds began their magic. Within an hour, the Matterhorn was revealed. And it was a sight to behold! Sort of. Austin verbalized what we were all thinking: "You know, I'm a bit disappointed. I expected more. This is incredible, but I thought it was going to be so much more."

Well, I just had to capture what I saw as a "teachable moment," even if my son was now an adult. So we sat there talking about the buildups and letdowns of life. Unrushed, we enjoyed our hot chocolate and good conversation. And the whole time, unnoticed by us, the winds kept moving.

Austin became less absorbed by our conversation and more absorbed in what was happening farther off. "Mom, Dad, what is that?" he exclaimed. Looking up, I honestly had no idea what the clouds had now revealed. Hadn't we already seen the Matterhorn?

Austin's smile said it all. What we had assumed was the Matterhorn was only a small ridge. Our decision to sit and talk had allowed time for the winds to reveal the greatness of the true Matterhorn. It was more spectacular than we could have imagined!

I thought of the apostle Paul's words in Ephesians 3:20: "Now all glory to God, who is able, through his mighty power at work within us, to accomplish infinitely more than we might ask or think" (NLT). Infinitely more. That's what the Matterhorn was. And that's what I wanted my life to be—abundantly alive!

Perhaps you are already enjoying spiritual abundance and can't imagine a better life than the one you are living. Or perhaps *abundance* is far removed from any word you'd use to describe your life. Whatever your circumstances or season, your Matterhorn awaits you—a life with God far better than you can imagine.

All the tour guides assured us that the Matterhorn would live up to its promises, and all the passages assure us that God will live up to *His* promises. Do you know God's promises for your life? Here are just a few of many.

- He has a plan and a purpose for you, meaningful work for you to do.

- Not only can He heal your past and present hurts and failures, but He can also use them to deliver His hope to those who are still without hope.

- He will turn the shame you bear into gain and your disgrace into dignity.

I know, I know. It sounds too good to be true. But it isn't. I've seen firsthand that the Matterhorn is more majestic than I could have imagined. Likewise, I have experienced firsthand that God's purposes for me are more amazing than I could have imagined.

God is waiting for you to offer Him all that you are today—the good and the bad, your strengths and your weaknesses—so that He can make you all that He knows you *can be*. His power will utterly transform you, accomplishing in and through you things infinitely greater than you could imagine. Do you dare to believe? I encourage you to take those first steps of faith and experience for yourself all God has planned for you.

~ ~ ~ ~

As with so much else in life, forethought is required. I challenge you to:

- *Plan purposefully.* Establish in advance your time and place for these devotionals. Have your Bible handy, a journal, and a pen or pencil.

- *Prepare prayerfully.* Ask God to personalize each day's reading to your circumstances, needs, and dreams.

- *Proceed positively.* Expect God to do great things in the next forty days. Expect the unexpected. Anything you could imagine will fall short of what God has in mind.

- *Pursue persistently.* Don't give up. You will encounter all kinds of obstacles, including an enemy who does not want you to stay the course and receive the blessings God has for you. But if you expect distractions, then you will not be caught off guard and will stay steady in your determination to finish well.

Are you ready? A little nervous? That's normal. The effort involved to obtain anything worth having is both exhilarating and unsettling. Let's not waste time on fears and excuses. Let's get started! God is waiting to reveal all He has created you to be.

DAY 1

Pearls

Now all glory to God, who is able, through his mighty power at work within us, to accomplish infinitely more than we might ask or think.

Once upon a time, there was a little girl with a pearl necklace. She loved her pearls even though they were only imitation pearls. Each evening her dad would read her a bedtime story, and then he would look at his little princess and ask, "Do you love me enough to give me those pearls?" The little girl would squirm nervously and tuck the pearls behind her back, holding on because she loved them ever so much.

The same routine continued for many months. One evening, as her dad closed the book, he asked again, "Do you love me enough to give me your pearls?" Would the little girl dare to offer all she had—all that brought her comfort, all that she loved so dearly—to her father? After a long, thoughtful pause, and trying desperately to hold back tears, the little girl slowly brought her hand from behind her back and spilled forth the tarnished strand of pearls.

Her tears of sadness soon turned to tears of delight as she saw why her dad had been asking all along for her treasure. His intent was not to take it away from her, but to offer a greater treasure in exchange. For from his hands into hers slid a new strand of *real* pearls.

What "imitation pearls" are you grasping ever so tightly? What are the things this world says should make you happy but instead leave you feeling empty? What imitation treasures hinder you from experiencing a greater treasure?

When God first spoke to me through Ephesians 3:20, He issued this challenge: Would I dare to hand over my imitation pearls in exchange for a life of "infinitely more"? I said yes, and now I'm sharing with you the discoveries I've made so far. I welcome you along—discoveries are more fun with companions! I know without a doubt that God is going to reveal Himself to you in new ways over the next forty days and beyond.

I hope you will journal about your discoveries, your thoughts, what God is saying to you, and your prayers. It makes the journey even richer. For today's journal entry, try to identify some "imitation pearls" in your life—those things you treasure far more than their true value merits. Perhaps you will want to add to the list in the days ahead as God reveals more pearls in your life. Your list is between you and God, so be honest, be brave, be *you*. Then begin a habit of asking Him daily, "What is the *infinitely more* you want to give me today?"

DAY 2

Could This Be the Day?

Now all glory to God, who is able, through his mighty power at work within us, to accomplish infinitely more than we might ask or think.

Ephesians 3:20 intimidated me at first with its call to live beyond anything I know I can accomplish. But it also promised that whatever God called me to would be possible through *His* power at work within me. That promised power gave me the confidence to make this my "life verse"—a verse that continuously guides and impacts how I live.

What is God asking you to do today? What have you been putting off? I know what it's like to keep saying, *One day, God, one day*. But ask yourself, *Could one day be* this *day?*

"A year from now you may wish you had started today" (author unknown). Pause in this thought, and ask God what He wants to tell you about His next step for you—the step beyond what you know is possible. Where does He want to take you that is beyond your own strength, talents, willpower, and abilities? What do you really want to do but are not sure is possible? Matthew 19:26 records Jesus saying, "With man this is impossible, but with God all things are possible." Imagine Jesus saying these words directly to you today. How does that change your perspective on what lies ahead of you?

In your journal, write down your conversation with God—the fears you admit to Him, the dreams you describe to Him, the limitations that keep you from believing He can do amazing things in and through you. If you're intimidated by what God has planned for you, tell Him so. And then wait a bit. What words does He whisper to your heart? Be sure to write down His part of the conversation as well.

DAY 3

Stuck in the Right Place

Now all glory to God, who is able, through his mighty power at work within us, to accomplish infinitely more than we might ask or think.

As I sit at my computer this morning, I can't stop thinking about the many challenges my friends face. A woman in Montana is helping a relative endure intense chemotherapy. A teenager nervously anticipates a new school. Some friends are worried about their children. Another is waking up from surgery. Many are going off to stressful work environments, or searching in vain for any work at all. Others face legal battles or drawn-out medical treatments. And then there are the "ordinary" challenges: how to be a better friend, how to be kinder to a spouse, how to juggle competing time demands. You know what I'm talking about, don't you!

How would God tell us to begin a day like this? His answer may seem more difficult than our circumstances!

> *Always be joyful. Never stop praying. Be thankful in all circumstances, for this is God's will for you who belong to Christ Jesus. (1 Thessalonians 5:16–18 NLT)*

Is God kidding? His will is that we be joyful, pray, and give thanks? Are you shaking your head in disbelief, finding it hard to be the tiniest bit joyful? Does it seem impossible to offer even a syllable of thanks? Then I suppose you are stuck.

But wait a minute: That's not a bad place to be. In fact, that's great place to be. For according to these verses, when you are stuck between joy and thanksgiving, it means you are praying, and that means you are right in the middle of God's will. See the progression: Be joyful, *never stop praying,* be thankful.

On a day like today, when we're burdened with the weight of life's challenges, prayer is a tremendous gift. Who can anticipate how a day's worth of prayer might alter the saddest of circumstances? Prayer changes things. Can that thought alone bring you a smidgen of joy? Can it make you thankful? You'll never know until you try. So grab that pen and pour your heart out to God in your journal. Let Him know about your friends who need burdens lifted today. Let Him know about the burdens you carry this day.

Wait. What's that? Could it be joy?

DAY 4

Relationally Speaking

*Now all glory to God, who is able,
through his mighty power at work within us,
to accomplish infinitely more than we
might ask or think.*

As I came around the corner from my daily run, the sight of full-bloom crepe myrtles took my breath away. When we first planted them in our yard, I feared that the scrawny limbs would not live. I never dreamed they would burst forth with such an abundance of beauty.

I immediately thought of Isaiah 42:5: "[It is God] who created the heavens and stretched them out, who spread forth the earth and that which comes from it" (NKJV). *That's our God,* I thought. With just a word from Him all things were created (including crepe myrtles), and with His word the impossible is made possible.

For so many years, the second part of that truth confused me more than comforted me. If, with one word, God could prevent all these hurts and heal all pain and injustice, why would He not do that? It took a long while, but I finally realized that with God, it's more relational than situational.

God tucks relational opportunities amid each day's "impossible" situations. Look around you today. Whom do you see? With whom have you bonded because of your circumstances? You may not want to be in the situation you find yourself today, but God has placed you there and trusts you to reach those you would not otherwise have the opportunity to reach.

God has plans today for your relationships. With that in mind, think about the relationships entwined with your troubling and seemingly impossible situations. Spend some time talking with God about them. Ask Him to open your eyes to see His purposes in each relationship. Write down any insights He gives you as you talk with Him. Then get out there and start relating!

DAY 5

What a Masterpiece!

Now all glory to God, who is able, through his mighty power at work within us, to accomplish infinitely more than we might ask or think.

One day Michelangelo was working on a huge rock with his hammer and chisel. He was in the beginning stages of transforming it into a work of art. A man came along and asked with a smirk, "Why are you wasting your time on that ugly rock?"

Michelangelo replied, "I see a beautiful angel trapped in this rock, and I'm doing my best to let him out."

Do you know what your Master Artist sees when He looks at you today? Someone even you cannot see or imagine!

When others looked at Simon the fisherman, they saw a presumptuous, opinionated, hotheaded, and self-centered man. But God knew He could chisel out of the rough rock named Simon a great man who would become Peter. And only the Lord could see beyond the fearful, whiney, excuse-making Gideon to His future masterpiece—a "mighty warrior."

Understand this: God chooses you as you are presently—but He also sees you as you will be potentially. Man looks, judges, and chooses based on outward appearances, but God has already chosen you because He sees your heart for Him.

If you awoke today feeling like an ugly rock, then Ephesians 2:10 will brighten your day. It says that you are God's workmanship (masterpiece!), created in Christ Jesus with the promise that you will do good works. God has put more into you and sees more in you than you can imagine. By your steadfast belief in God's word today, or by the simplicity of a kind response to a hurting stranger, you can reveal the incredible work He has already accomplished in you.

Let this good news shape your conversation with God today. Don't shrug it off as "happy talk." If the thought of yourself as a masterpiece is hard to accept, admit those feelings in your journal. But also ask God to help you comprehend the magnificent potential He sees in you. Then step into today's Ephesians 3:20 promise with fresh faith and confidence.

DAY 6

Called to Encourage

Now all glory to God, who is able, through his mighty power at work within us, to accomplish infinitely more than we might ask or think.

Peter is one of my favorite guys in the Bible. Some say he was an egomaniac. Some call him impulsive. Others point out his hair-trigger temper. Whatever others saw, Jesus saw Peter's heart and passion. Jesus chose Peter as he was presently, but Jesus also saw Peter's potential. To fulfill that potential, however, Peter needed encouragement. Otherwise he would easily be sidelined by the mistakes that lay ahead in his life.

> *And the Lord said, "Simon, Simon! Indeed, Satan has asked for you, that he may sift you as wheat. But I have prayed for you, that your faith should not fail; and when you have returned to Me, strengthen your brethren."*
> *(Luke 22:31–32 NKJV)*

As Jesus faced death, He pulled Peter aside to strengthen and prepare him for what was about to happen. Jesus knew Peter's loyalty would be severely tested, so He expressed confidence that, even though Peter's faith would falter, it would not be fatal. Peter's mistakes would make him stronger and equip him to strengthen others.

During your Ephesians 3:20 journey, you will discover that God wants to use you "infinitely more" than you could imagine to support and encourage others. No matter how busy your life, strengthening others for their journeys is one of the most important ministries you could practice.

In your journal today, write the names of a few people you sense could use encouragement. Ask God to show you how you can strengthen them—through a note or email, a phone call, a small gift, or some gesture you'd never have thought of on your own. Later, record in your journal what you did and how the person responded. Thank God for allowing you to share in His ministry of encouragement and support.

Encourage one another daily,
as long as it is called "Today."
(Hebrews 3:13)

DAY 7

Need a Miracle?

Now all glory to God, who is able, through his mighty power at work within us, to accomplish infinitely more than we might ask or think.

Yesterday I followed my usual routine. Rolled out of bed before dawn. Grabbed my coffee. Headed to the computer. Sat. Prayed. Wrote.

I was satisfied with what I had written and ready to post it online, but an uneasiness told me God was about to critique what I'd written—which, by the way, is awesome but time consuming. Didn't God know I was on a tight schedule? Finally, with the revisions made, I was ready to hit "send" when the computer shut down. All my work was lost! I needed a miracle!

We all know what to do in situations like this: Pray! And so I began: *Dear Jesus, please, please, please save this! Please help me get this out!*

(Computer still down.) *Dear Lord, I know you have called me to write; I know this is your will. Please help me!*

(Computer dead.) *Dear Jesus, please restore this computer now!*

(Is there such a state as "deader"?) *OK, Lord, you know I have done all that you have asked of me. I got up early. I tried my best. I ... I ... I ...*

Sound familiar? Are you in a situation larger than your capabilities? Are you doing all you feel

God is requiring of you, and yet nothing seems to be happening? Have you tried mending a relationship for years without results? Or tried forgiving someone again and again and continue to struggle? Are you, like I was, feeling frustrated and confused, tempted to give up but determined not to because the task at hand is too important to abandon?

Convinced my work was lost, I cried out, *What in the world should I do now?* Then a message appeared on my screen: Mail Waiting to Be Sent. Huh? How could that happen with the computer down?

I can't tell you how that happened, but I can tell you this: God hasn't shut down on you. He may seem silent, but He is there. He is right in the middle of your situation and your dreams. Today. Now. All your hard work, all your obedience to Him, all the hours you have prayed, and even your secret tears have not gone unnoticed by Him. If you believe what you are praying is God's will, and you believe you are doing what God is asking, then abandon yourself to God's timing and know He is still in the miracle business. Your miracle, like my email, is waiting to be sent.

In the meantime, God says, "Let us not become weary in doing good, for at the proper time we will reap a harvest if we do not give up" (Galatians 6:9). Write a prayer to Him in your journal today, telling Him how much that assurance means to you.

DAY 8

You Are Here

Now all glory to God, who is able, through his mighty power at work within us, to accomplish infinitely more than we might ask or think.

You Are Here. These three words on the mall directory relieved my fatigue and frustration. I knew my destination, but I also had to know where I *was* to get to where I wanted to be. Three little words did the trick.

Perhaps by now your Ephesians 3:20 journey has you feeling a little lost and fatigued. When this happens, knowing *who* you are—instead of *where* you are—will take you where you need to be.

In Isaiah 42:1, God says, "Here is my servant, whom I uphold, my chosen one in whom I delight." Jesus was proclaimed the Chosen One, and you've been chosen too. Now, when God chooses you, He also loves you and delights in you—today and every day. You never leave His mind, escape His sight, or flee from His thoughts. Because He is not restricted by time, every day and deed of your past, present, and future have passed before His eyes. Even your future failings, struggles, and sins have been taken into account. He knows and understands you better than you know yourself. And yet His resolve remains the same: He loves you! He delights in you. You can do nothing to make Him love you more, and you can do nothing to cause Him to love you less.

Put another way: The overwhelmingly good news is not that you love God; it is that He loves you! Not that you have found God (though that is good), but that in Him you have been found. As the directory says, *You Are Here.*

God has promised, through His mighty power at work within you, to accomplish infinitely more than you might ask or think. But be warned: You will have days when you feel lost. Fatigue and frustration will set in. When they do, run to this devotion as your spiritual directory. Find it and be encouraged by allowing God to remind you that *you are here*:

- Called by Him.

- Chosen by Him.

- Upheld by Him.

- The one in whom He delights.

You are right where you need to be to have immediate access to His enduring strength, wisdom, and rest. Use your journaling time today to describe how knowing that *you are here* changed your perspective on today's events and encounters.

DAY 9

Declaration of Hope

Now all glory to God, who is able, through his mighty power at work within us, to accomplish infinitely more than we might ask or think.

I will never forget watching the news report on South Carolina First Lady Jenny Sanford's divorce-driven departure from the governor's mansion. The cameras hovered intrusively for a glimpse of what Mrs.

Sanford later referred to as her "most excruciating day of pain."

As she exited through the mansion's majestic gates into a sea of reporters, I marveled at her courage. Relentless questions flew at her: "What will you do now?" "How will you survive?" "How embarrassing is this to you?" "How will you explain this to your boys?" "How did it feel to hear your husband declaring another woman as his soul mate?"

Ms. Sanford acknowledged her agony and devastation. She conceded the path before her was not clear and would be walked one day—and one gut-wrenching decision—at a time. But amidst her pain she also proclaimed confidence that her path would lead to rebuilding and healing, and that she and her boys would "not only survive, but would thrive."

As believers, we are called not only to survive devastation in our lives, but to be better because of it. That's when the world sees much more than a group of good little people; the world sees a God who is bigger than anything we might have to handle.

Take a moment to ponder your life and its hurts. Record some words in your journal that describe the pain you've lived through, the burdens you still carry. Now think about how acknowledging your faith amidst your pain today can inspire those around you. What might happen if you allow God to use your secret pain to bring hope to others who hurt? Write a prayer in your journal, asking God to lead you to someone today who needs to hear you proclaim the kind of hope Jenny Sanford declared.

DAY 10

Heavenly Setups

Now all glory to God, who is able,
through his mighty power at work within us,
to accomplish infinitely more than we
might ask or think.

Be assured that a plan is unfolding in your life today. You may think you chose your home because of the good deal, picked that class just for the teacher, received your job on your own merits, or ran back into the store because you forgot the sugar. But beyond the obvious, you'll find other reasons. I call these reasons "heavenly setups."

Don't we all suspect—deep down inside—that what we do and where we go in life has a deeper meaning than is apparent from one day to the next? Proverbs 20:24 tells us, "A person's steps are directed by the LORD." To fulfill our roles as we follow in those steps, we are told to "make the most of every opportunity" (Colossians 4:5). So, I guess the question is: As you run back through the store, master your job, and walk your neighborhood, how can you touch the lives of those God has placed before you?

It begins with a simple look.

All around you—in the lines at the store, in the cubicles at your office, in the bleachers at each game—are those who silently hurt. Their smiles may be intact, but look more carefully. See beyond those darling shoes. Look deep into their eyes. Look at everyone through the hurts you currently bear. What do you see? The pain of rejection? Worry? Fear? The devastation of an unraveling marriage or an unsettled teen. Addiction or just plain emptiness? Who is silently screaming for help? Who is trying to find the "more" in life? You can choose to be used today beyond anything you can imagine by first looking and then asking, "How are you really?"

Read the quote by Henri Nouwen that follows, and write in your journal whatever comes to your mind as you think of the words *wounded healer.* Are these positive or negative words to you? How do they tie in with other things you've been learning on your Ephesians 3:20 journey? How do you feel about embracing the role of wounded healer as part of God's unfolding plan for you?

Nobody escapes being wounded. We all are wounded people, whether physically, emotionally, mentally, or spiritually. The main question is not "How can we hide our wounds?" so we don't have to be embarrassed, but "How can we put our woundedness in the service of others?" When our wounds cease to be a source of shame, and become a source of healing, we have become wounded healers. (Henri Nouwen, The Wounded Healer*)*

DAY 11

Glorious Giggles

Now all glory to God, who is able, through his mighty power at work within us, to accomplish infinitely more than we might ask or think.

A friend of mine wages a great battle. Indescribable hurt and devastation have been unjustly heaped upon her family. Only God, her family, and her best friend know her deep turmoil and agony. Only they could speak adequately of the sleepless nights and spent tears. Yet my friend fights like a mama bear. And in the midst of the battle, she insists on protecting her family's "joking time" and finding reasons to laugh together.

My friend brings to mind Proverbs 17:22: "A cheerful heart is good medicine."

Before heading out to whatever your day holds, follow her lead and take a good dose of Proverbs 17:22. Research shows that laughing will not only reduce your stress, but will also increase your tolerance for pain, release infection-fighting antibodies, boost your attentiveness, and accelerate your energy. Good medicine, indeed.

Beyond all that, finding a reason to giggle today can glorify God. It proclaims to those who hear you that you believe—through His mighty power at work in you, and in each circumstance and situation that touches your life—He is about to accomplish more than you have asked or even thought to ask!

So giggle. And before you go to bed tonight, take time to describe in your journal something that made your heart cheerful today. In fact, you might want to make a "Laugh List" a nightly habit. Wouldn't it be fun to hit the pillow with your head filled with memories of the day's laughter!

DAY 12

An Amazing Story

Now all glory to God, who is able, through his mighty power at work within us, to accomplish infinitely more than we might ask or think.

The life of Joseph (told in Genesis 30–50) is a story of extreme highs and extreme lows that took him from favorite son, to the pit, to the prison, and, finally, to the palace.

What amazes me is that I can see God at work from the story's beginning until its final chapter. But then again, I know how the story is going to end. I doubt Joseph found it as amazing as he lived it from day to day, wondering what was going to happen next. One day, deeply honored by his father; the next day, betrayed, deserted, and sold into slavery by his brothers. One day, promoted for doing great things; the next, punished for doing the right thing.

We all have moments when we wonder what in the world is going on. We cannot see the next chapter in our story like we can see the next chapter in Joseph's story. So, let's do what Joseph did: Let's choose to believe God is working for our good in today's situation, whether we're in the pit or the palace. One day our children, or their children or those who knew us best, will look back at the story we left behind and be amazed. They will be able to see how

God was at work all along, accomplishing a greater outcome than anyone ever dared to imagine.

Take time today to tell God in your journaling about a situation that feels like a pit to you. Then express your commitment to believe that He is at work in that situation, and the outcome will be amazing.

DAY 13

Unbelievable

Now all glory to God, who is able, through his mighty power at work within us, to accomplish infinitely more than we might ask or think.

Many great men and women in the Bible had occasions when they could not figure out what God was up to.

Abraham could not understand why God would ask Him to give up what he loved most in the world.

Moses could not understand why God would keep him wandering in the wilderness for forty years. And dear Mary and Martha tried desperately to understand why Jesus lingered when their brother Lazarus was dying.

What in your life leaves you dumbfounded? What dream is dying? What seems unfair? What do you long for that God seems to be withholding? Perhaps God has brought you to this place to prepare you for His next miracle in your life.

The saying goes, "You gotta believe!" Within those three words lies the secret to unleashing the power of Ephesians 3:20 in your life today. The world proclaims, "You need to see to believe." But Jesus declares just the opposite. He says, "Believe, then you will see" (see John 11:40).

Today, you may not understand your situation but will you declare a renewed belief that from that situation God is preparing to call forth your very own miracle? It may be a miracle of healing or restoration; a miracle of strength or favor; a miracle of salvation or exoneration; or the miracle of a job, forgiveness, patience, or kindness. Begin this day praying for and believing in your miracle! Write down your declaration of belief in your journal.

DAY 14

Is Your God Able?

Now all glory to God, who is able, through his mighty power at work within us, to accomplish infinitely more than we might ask or think.

Yesterday we saw that believing is the secret to unleashing God's power in our lives. I don't know about you, but for the longest time, I thought, *OK, but what exactly am I to believe?*

Jesus answers this question with Mary and Martha. By the time Jesus arrived in response to their pleas, Lazarus had died. The sisters were overwhelmed by grief, agonizing questions, and a sense of betrayal.

Yet Jesus was well aware of the circumstances. He had already told His disciples, "Lazarus is dead, and for your sake I am glad I was not there, so that you may believe" (John 11:14–15). He entered Lazarus's situation knowing exactly what He was going to do. He enters your situation today in the same way. You may think He is too late, but He is right on time. Even though you feel overlooked or forgotten, He is about to bring great and lasting gain to you. However, what He has to say may seem outrageous. To Martha, Jesus proclaimed that her dead brother would live. But then Jesus looked directly at Martha with the deeper belief issue. He said, "I am the resurrection and the life. ... Do you believe this?" (John 11:23–25).

Jesus was going beyond Martha's circumstances to the condition of her heart. "Do you believe in Me?" He was asking. "Do you believe I am able?"

Standing in the face of your impossibility, the death of your dream, the death of your reputation, the death of your finances or your marriage, the death of _____ (you fill in the blank), Jesus knows exactly what He will do. But first He wants to know what you believe. He is asking you, "Do you believe I am able?"

Martha responded, "Yes, Lord, ... I believe." How do you respond in your daily life?

In your journal, list the "impossibilities" in your life that you are struggling to entrust to Jesus. Be honest with Him about your doubts and unbelief by praying as the distraught father prayed in Mark 9:24:

"I do believe; help me overcome my unbelief!" Then sit in silence for a while and let God speak words of courage to your heart. In these sorts of conversations with Him, your unbelief will steadily transform itself to belief.

DAY 15

The Power of Thankfulness

Now all glory to God, who is able, through his mighty
power at work within us, to accomplish infinitely
more than we might ask or think.

I have always loved the praise and worship segment
of our church services. But my boys—not so much.
Sunday after Sunday, unrelentingly, I would nudge,

elbow, whatever I could to encourage them to participate. Finally, one of my guys looked at me and said, "We may not be singing on the outside, Mom, but we are singing in our hearts."

For many people, maybe even you, thankfulness and praise do not flow easily. Perhaps you're uncomfortable with expressing yourself in song. Maybe you simply can't find much for which you are thankful.

This was the case with Mary and Martha. As we return to the tomb of Lazarus, we see these sisters spewing their disappointment to Jesus. But Jesus told them, "The one who believes in me will live" (John 11:25). He was showing them that the secret to unleashing God's power began with believing: believing in Him, believing in His word, believing that He is able to accomplish what He says He can do.

But Jesus does something else to bring life in the face of death:

They took the stone away.
Then Jesus looked up and said,
"Father, I thank you that you
have heard me." (John 11:41)

First, He looks up.

And then He gives thanks.

Jesus has brought you to the place of your next miracle. And you can unleash God's miracle-making power today by believing and then by proclaiming your thanksgiving.

Look up! If nothing else, you can be thankful today that God hears you: "This is the confidence we have in approaching God: ... he hears us" (1 John 5:14).

Write in your journal "15 Reasons to Give Thanks on Day 15." I've already given you the first reason: God hears you. Now add fourteen other things for which to be thankful.

DAY 16

To the Giver's Glory

Now all glory to God, who is able, through his mighty power at work within us, to accomplish infinitely more than we might ask or think.

With no rain forecasted, Lee and I planned a trip to the beach. Can you guess what happened? Yep, down came the rain! Yet we felt a strange pull to stay the course. So, through horrendous traffic, plummeting rain, thunder, and lightning, off we went. Seven hours into our trip, with no end of the rain and only backed-up traffic in sight, we decided to give up and turn around. Unknown to us, we stopped at just the right place to meet members of the Virginia Fire 13U baseball team.

"Ma'am, would you like to buy some donuts?" asked a young lad. His team was raising funds to attend a tournament. I handed over what little cash I had. What happened next transformed an ordinary encounter into the extraordinary.

The team had been making money since early morning; my contribution was neither their first nor their largest, but you would have thought I had given the moon. Thankfulness beamed from this little guy's eyes. He grinned from ear to ear and gave me a big thumbs-up. "We're gonna win just for you!" he declared.

The giver of so little, I had been given so much.

James tells us that "Every good and perfect gift is from above, coming down from the Father" (1:17). Driving home that day, I was reminded of all the gifts I receive daily. This little team had motivated me to exhibit their "glory to God" kind of thankfulness.

So Caleb, Mason, Drew, Collin, Corey, Shawn, Spencer, Dari, Doray, Chase, Thomas, and Ed—I return a big thumbs-up, and I thank you for reminding me of the real challenge of Ephesians 3:20. Yes, we must believe and give thanks, but all for one reason: to give glory to our Giver, the One who gave His all to ensure us an abundant life of victory.

Add another reason to give thanks to your journal today!

DAY 17

Memories of Encouragement

Now all glory to God, who is able, through his mighty power at work within us, to accomplish infinitely more than we might ask or think.

Listen to how Paul begins his second letter of encouragement to Timothy: "I thank God, whom I serve, ... I constantly remember you in my prayers. ... I long to see you, so that I may be filled with joy. I am reminded of your sincere faith" (2 Timothy 1:3–5).

These two had been through a lot together: wonderful, celebratory times and dark, agonizing times. Their faith in God and belief in one another had allowed them to survive and bonded them in such a way that, even when they were separated, their memories brought joy, strength, and encouragement.

In your embrace of Ephesians 3:20, God is leading you to "new things" (see Isaiah 42:9). It's like Christmas Eve—knowing gifts are waiting and wondering what you are about to be given—don't you think? What is the "infinitely more" God has wrapped and is ready to deliver next in the plan He has declared for you? How exciting to contemplate the new thing He is preparing to do for and through you!

It seems to me, however, that God wants to pull you aside for just a day or two—perhaps to give rest, but also to strengthen you with reminders of all the special people He has placed in your life. John Maxwell says, "Believing in people before they have succeeded is the key to motivating them to reach their fullest potential."

Who has believed in you and motivated you toward your Christ-given potential? List their names in your journal. Spend some time thanking God for each person. Before this day ends, send at least one of those people an email or note to thank them for the role they have played in your life.

DAY 18

A Promising Outcome

Now all glory to God, who is able, through his mighty power at work within us, to accomplish infinitely more than we might ask or think.

WARNING: Disappointments, hurts, trials, and even tribulations are coming your way.

PROMISE: That's not the end of your story.

Jesus is very up-front with us in John 16:33. He doesn't paint a rosy picture, but He *does* proclaim a promising outcome. He quickly transforms bad news into good—and compels us to action. "Take heart," He says, "I have overcome the world." He will have the final say about all your disappointments and hurts.

What hope this brings to any situation you may face today! God always has the final word about your life. And His final word today is this: He can turn to your good the hurt that is intended as evil against you; He can replace the shame you bear with double gain; and He can replace your disgrace with an inheritance, namely His mighty promises (see Isaiah 61:7).

Hold on, I believe He whispers to you today, *your blessing is coming. More than you can picture and in greater ways than you can imagine.*

You know by now that disappointments are inevitable, but your response does not need to be discouragement. You can instead take heart right now, this minute, by letting go of the fear that you are hoping and trusting in vain. One more time, declare God is able! And because He is able, the end of your matter will be better than its beginning (see Ecclesiastes 7:8).

Imagine that your journal is a huge tote bag. Fill it with the fears, disappointments, and hurts you are carrying around today. But don't stop there. Imagine yourself reaching into your ridiculously heavy bag of troubles and handing each one to God. Take a deep breath of relief as you let each burden go. Draw a line through each burden in your bag as you release it to God. Then walk into your day knowing that your cares and concerns are in good hands.

DAY 19

Who Knows?

Now all glory to God, who is able, through his mighty power at work within us, to accomplish infinitely more than we might ask or think.

Who really knows you? Who knows the challenges you face today? Who understands your loneliness? Who knows how you ache because of the loss you just suffered? Who knows how terrified you are? Who knows your financial distress, the hidden addiction, the depression lingering behind the big smile and cute shoes? Who knows that you are barely holding on? Who knows not only the complications of your life, but, more importantly, the state of your heart?

Jesus knows.

At the death of their brother Lazarus, Jesus wept with Mary and Martha. He cried with them in their deepest despair and loss. Don't take this as an act of weakness. Don't think He didn't know how to handle the situation or was not in control of it. Jesus knew what was about to happen; He had come to restore life to Lazarus. He knew the miracle He was there to perform, yet He cared so deeply for Mary and Martha that He sat with them, He listened, and He wept.

He sits with you today, and He has sent a friend to sit with you. Someone cares and is ready to listen. You know who they are, don't you?

I've found that to release the flow of God's power in my life, I first have to allow the truth of my life to flow. I have to let people know the real me. Recently, I sat with a group of women I call friends and shared with them about a time long ago when I began asking a lot of the above questions. God, in his infinite care, sent the friends; I had to find the courage to share myself with them.

Today, run to God. "Cast all your anxiety on him because he cares for you" (1 Peter 5:7). And then run to the phone and call that person you know you can trust. She is never going to know the real you until you find the courage to share. By beginning the conversation, you will also allow your friend to begin her long-awaited conversation with you. If you are truly ready to see God's power at work within you in ways you could not begin to imagine, then this is your starting place today. And your journal can be a place where you track the growth of your new friendship and marvel at what God is doing. Pick up that phone right now!

DAY 20

We Need to Talk

Now all glory to God, who is able, through his mighty power at work within us, to accomplish infinitely more than we might ask or think.

Sitting in the back pew of the chapel, I grew more and more anxious. I had flown into Phoenix to interview a prospective musical trio for my conferences. Now I was wondering how I had gotten myself into this mess. Little did I know that from this "mess" I was about to hear God's powerful message.

I wept as I watched women, from their teens to their seventies, struggle to their seats. Many slumped with exhaustion or rested on a neighbor's shoulder. Some were so thin that I wondered what kept their bones from tearing through their skin. Bald patches, sunken eyes, feeding tubes, wheelchairs—this is where life had brought them. And now God had brought me to a world-renowned treatment center for people with eating disorders.

I knew the lies these women had believed. I understood that each time they looked into the mirror they believed something other than God's truth about themselves. I knew all this because I had lived it too.

We all fight lies—that we are not smart enough, funny enough, or good enough; or that we are too marred by our sin to be usable or forgiven. We are tied to our past, fear blinds our future, and lies handcuff the possibilities of today. Not knowing what else to do, we smile and declare, "I'm fine."

Try this exercise: In your journal, write the words *I'm fine.* Then draw a line through the words. Now list what you truly believe about yourself: I'm unqualified. I'm not loveable. I'm unforgiven. I'm too fat/thin/young/old. I'm a failure. And so on.

I am convinced that the greatest thing your Ephesians 3:20 journey will accomplish is to give you courage to pursue true relationships—friendships in which you share the hard, dark truth with others. These friendships will help break the bondage of lies you've been telling yourself. In the weeks ahead, you will look back at today's journal entry and be able to strike out each lie and replace it with the truth. "I'm unlovable" will become "I am loved for exactly who I am." "I'm unforgiven" will be replaced with "Nothing can separate me from God's love, not even my sin."

God has done His part. It's time you do yours—with friends!

DAY 21

Misery Requires Company

Now all glory to God, who is able, through his mighty power at work within us, to accomplish infinitely more than we might ask or think.

Even the most spiritual person can be overwhelmed with loneliness.

Take Martha, for example, busy with the Lord's work, she felt she was the only one trying to please Jesus. Her loneliness fed a judgmental spirit and caused a verbal assault on her sister (see Luke 10:38–40).

And then there was Elijah in 1 Kings 17–19. This great prophet raised the widow's son from the dead and defeated the prophets of Baal at Carmel. A spiritual giant, wouldn't you say? Yet he ran away like a scaredy-cat after a woman named Jezebel threatened him. He fled into the wilderness, plopped down under a broom tree, and, overcome by depression, prayed that God would take his life.

We all need somebody—and not just anybody. Not just a shopping buddy or a spa-day pal or a tennis or golf partner, but somebody who really knows us. Because we'll all have moments like Martha's and days like Elijah's. We're going to get stuck or all wadded up because of something that was said or done—even during our Ephesians 3:20 journey! We

can learn from Martha and Elijah and choose a different path—the path to a good friend.

Conversation with a trusted friend is not proof
that misery loves company, but rather that misery
requires company. Within open, honest conversation,
the blinders will fall away from your eyes allowing
you to see that you are not alone.

> *Two are better than one…*
> *If either of them falls down,*
> *one can help the other up.*
> *(Ecclesiastes 4:9–10)*

Think about it. Would you rather spend the day
wallowing under a broom tree? Or would you rather
spend it with _____? Fill in the blank, make
the phone call, and then record in your journal how
the visit with your friend turned out. Did you indeed
discover that two are better than one?

DAY 22

Pushing Buttons

Now all glory to God, who is able, through his mighty power at work within us, to accomplish infinitely more than we might ask or think.

I love writing. The discipline and challenge have changed my life. Being out of town, however, makes my writing routine more challenging. Normally I get up early and write, and then I slip into my old running shoes for my special time with God. It's not study time; it's "God and me" time—relaxing, talking, and listening time. It's also where, so often, I get hints about the next day's writing topic.

Because my motto is "When you mess up, you fess up," I will "fess up" to you my "mess up." Recently, while out of town, I didn't run.

On this particular morning, as I made my way down the hall to the hotel elevator, my head was full of chatter. *Now what is the message for today? What am I to write? I cannot believe I didn't run! I won't let this happen again. This is a mess. WAIT A MINUTE! How long have I been in this elevator?*

Yep, there I was in the beautiful mountains of North Carolina on a glorious Sunday morning, stuck in an elevator. All I could do was giggle at my foolishness. I had been standing there God-only-knows how long. Stuck because I hadn't pushed a button! And then I realized that once again, from within my mess, God had given me His message.

Being stuck in that silly elevator is a lot like the paralysis we can find ourselves in when we worry too much about what *we* have done, or have not done, or are going to do—and rely too little on what *God* is able to do. So today, give yourself a break and quit worrying. While it's true you are to live worthy of God's calling, you are not perfect. You're going to fail, but your failings have no power to stop God's will in your life. Just as I finally pushed the elevator's button to continue my journey, so you can push the button of His truth and experience the joy that promises to keep you moving forward.

Where is your elevator stuck this morning? Write the verse below in your journal—put it in your own words, if you'd like—as a way of pushing the button and moving into the day.

Being confident of this, that he who began a good work in you will carry it on to completion.
(Philippians 1:6)

DAY 23

Dream a Little Dream

Now all glory to God, who is able, through his mighty power at work within us, to accomplish infinitely more than we might ask or think.

"Dreams for Sale." I read the enticing message on a billboard as we left North Carolina.

If, within the next few days, you were granted the power to buy your dream, what would that dream be? If you were given a magic wand to wave over your circumstances, how would things change? Perhaps you would magically mend a relationship. Or buy healing of the emotional pain you carry that no one else can see. Would you want a spiritual change, maybe an end to the anger you feel toward God? Or perhaps, with a wave of the wand, you would acquire the material things you long for or desperately need. Would your magic wand have you winning a coveted trophy? Obtaining a more satisfying job? Getting into your dream school? Maybe your dream wouldn't be about you at all; maybe you long to see someone you love realize his or her dream. Whatever dreams come to mind as you read this paragraph, write them in your journal.

Now consider your Ephesians 3:20 truth: For anything you can dream this morning, God says He has "infinitely more" than you could ask, dare to think, or ever imagine.

Don't think that just because you didn't achieve your dreams that God has let you down. He's at work at this very moment doing something greater than the obvious, greater than you expect. Do you dare to believe this? Are you willing to pack up whatever belief you have this morning and travel deeper into this Ephesians journey with me? If you are, you will discover over the next few days that God has given you much more than a magic wand or the power to purchase your dreams. Are you ready for the trip?

Ready, set, STOP! (Day 24 will help you see why stopping allows God's plan to be fully achieved in your life.)

DAY 24

Ready, Set, What?

Now all glory to God, who is able, through his mighty power at work within us, to accomplish infinitely more than we might ask or think.

Ready, set, STOP! That's the message I left you with yesterday. I can imagine your reaction: What? Wait a minute! If I'm serious about seeing God do "infinitely more" than I could ask, dare to think, or even imagine, then shouldn't I go, go, go? Shouldn't the declaration this morning be "ready, set, GET BUSY!"?

The Bible indeed tells us to run, which means to be urgent about the work before us. But it also tells us to *prepare* for the run. One way we do that, according to Hebrews 12:1, is to "throw off everything that hinders."

What hinders you this day? What holds you back? Doubts? Fears? Worry? Do you think God is at work in everyone else, but you have grave doubts that He works in you? Do you feel unworthy? Do you think it may be too late? Maybe you just feel too busy with life. Maybe things have gotten so bad that you've concluded even God can't fix them. There's a wise saying that goes, "Where the mind leads, the man follows." Where has your mind been leading you as you have read these devotions for the last twenty-three days?

When calling Lazarus from the dead, Jesus said "Arise." He did not say, "Arise and run." He knew Lazarus' once-dead body would run again, just as He sees your running shoes lying there, waiting for the right moment. But first Lazarus had to be set free from the grave clothes that bound him. And we too have things we need to throw off each time we reach a new stage in our spiritual growth before the running can begin.

Jesus didn't call upon a magic wand to release Lazarus from his grave clothes; He called upon Lazarus's friends to prepare him to run. As your friend, I am going to help you prepare for the race in the days ahead. Let's start by naming in your journal the things that are hindering your progress right now. Maybe it's one big obstacle. Maybe it's an assortment of little, annoying hindrances. Name them. Then imagine yourself standing on the edge of a cliff, throwing those hindrances over the edge, one by one. How good that feels!

DAY 25

What Will They Think?

Now all glory to God, who is able, through his mighty
power at work within us, to accomplish infinitely
more than we might ask or think.

When I stepped outside for a run the other day, I
feared I might get cold in the brisk morning breeze.
So I grabbed a sweatshirt. Then I decided it was too
heavy. So I set off without it. A couple miles into my
run, I was thankful I had left the sweatshirt behind.

It would have really slowed me down, I remember thinking. And then I had my "ah ha" moment!

To properly explain, I should remind you of yesterday's question: *What holds you back?* The overwhelming answers I get when I ask women this question are worry and fear. We faithfully march on in the face of all kinds of political and economic uncertainty. But when it comes to sharing our *hearts*, we hesitate to take the next step.

Why? I believe it is because of the refrain "what will they think?" And "they" is not "the world." Our perceived threat of rejection, exposure, and abandonment comes from those who sit with us in church and in Bible study, those we call friends.

I recall the day (more than twenty years ago) when I first shared with a group of my friends some issues I was sure would send them running. Though I may have appeared "together" as their women's ministry leader, I was about to expose my secret pain of anorexia, anxiety attacks, and more. And this is what I learned: My friends cared *more* deeply for me after I shared. Those things I had tried so desperately to keep hidden were the very things God used to give my friends the freedom to share *their* fears and worries.

This is the message for today: We should be talking! Proverbs 12:25 says, "Anxiety weighs down the heart." What are you feeling weighed down by this morning? Write your worries and cares in your journal. Describe what scares you most about sharing these burdens with another person. Then ask God whom He wants you to talk with. You can be certain He has someone in mind.

DAY 26

An Invitation to Decline

Now all glory to God, who is able, through his mighty power at work within us, to accomplish infinitely more than we might ask or think.

Wouldn't it be wonderful to wake up without a care in the world? But let's face it, how often is that going to happen? We are tempted to worry before our feet even hit the floor. Yet there's hope. You see, temptations are merely invitations. We can choose to decline them.

Fear does not come from God. However, each time we are tempted to fear, God assures us of His faithfulness. So, tucked within each impulse to worry today lies a personal invitation: Choose fear or walk in faith. By choosing faith over fear, we receive these promises: We will never be tempted beyond what we can bear, and with each temptation God will provide a way out (see 1 Corinthians 10:13). What is the way out this morning as you face today's fears and worries?

Philippians 4:6 describes your escape route: "Do not be anxious about anything, but in every situation, by prayer and petition, with thanksgiving, present your requests to God."

This verse acknowledges that worries and fears are part of life. But it also shows you aren't stuck in those fears; you have been empowered to choose a better way. You can choose to release each worry and fear to the power of prayer. And then you can be thankful. Your thanksgiving declares that no matter your current circumstances, you believe God is actively working out "infinitely more" in your life than you can even imagine.

Fill your journal today with statements of release: *I release my fear of failure to you today, Lord. I release my worries about today's events, Lord.* And so on. Decline the invitation to cling to your concerns. Choose instead the invitation of Philippians 4:6.

DAY 27

Choose Life

Now all glory to God, who is able, through his mighty power at work within us, to accomplish infinitely more than we might ask or think.

"Choose life!" When I first read this directive in Deuteronomy 30:19, I snickered. Who wouldn't choose life? I was only thinking of one alternative to choosing life: choosing death. I wasn't considering that I could choose a life that was different from the one I was living.

You see, Jesus says He came not only to give us life, but to give us *abundant* life. Not just existence, getting by, or one more day at the office. No, He offers a life of abundance. This left me wondering if I was, in fact, choosing life.

The Greek word for abundance is *perissos,* and it means "exceeding, abundantly more, above or beyond." Where have we heard this before?

One of the great enemies of abundant living is worry. A national study concluded that 60 to 90 percent of doctor visits are stress related. Author and motivational speaker Earl Nightingale, when addressing "The Fog of Worry," suggested that 40 percent of what we worry about is wasted on things that will never come to pass. Thirty percent of our worries center on past decisions we cannot change while another 12 percent of our worries stem from the criticism of others—criticism often rooted more in the critic's sense of inferiority than in truth.*

So here's the question: What worries hinder you from choosing abundant life today? Picture this day as having two handles: the handle of fear and the handle of faith. In your journal create two columns. Label one column "The Handle of Fear," and list the fears and worries that are weighing you down right now. Label the other column "The Handle of Faith." List some of the truths you have been learning about God and His promises during your Ephesians 3:20 journey. Now, which handle will you choose today?

* Earl Nightingale, "The Fog of Worry (Only 8% of Worries Are Worth It)," Nightingale Conant, nightingale.com/articles/the-fog-of-worry-only-8-of-worries-are-worth-it/.

DAY 28

Temporary Status

Now all glory to God, who is able, through his mighty power at work within us, to accomplish infinitely more than we might ask or think.

We've seen how worry and fear hinder our Ephesians 3:20 journey. Here is another powerful hindrance: questioning if we are where we're supposed to be.

Do you ever wonder if you're in the right neighborhood? Right office? Right school? Are you even living in the right state? I struggled with such questions as we prepared to move from Augusta to Baltimore. I was leaving the comfort of friends, church, and routine, and closing the doors of my national women's ministry. I was taking my boys from a home and life they loved. It was more than I thought this mom's heart could endure. But with no other choice, we trudged ahead.

Within days of our arrival in Baltimore, I caught a glimmer of understanding. I was at the batting cages, watching my guys going on with life. They had uncertainties and fears about their new life, but they kept going. Soon I noticed them laughing and talking with someone I had earlier seen arriving alone. During their conversation, my guys learned their new friend had lost his family at a very young age. He had grown up without the simplest of things, like, for example, birthday celebrations and birthday cakes. As I saw my boys befriending him, I saw the light. It's not what we've been sent to get; it's what we've been sent to give.

That moment initiated a shift in my perspective about our move to Baltimore. And it introduced my family to someone who, to this day, remains very special in our lives.

Wherever you live, you're a temporary resident. But your temporary residencies will be filled with opportunities of eternal outcome. Fighting against where you are only distracts you from seeing what you have been sent there to do. You have been placed for a purpose. Even if you have questions and dismay and pain, you can choose to do what you can do, or give what you can give. This choice opens the door for God's power to continue His work within you—lifting you above the obstacles of unhappiness to the joy of being and doing "infinitely more" than you might ask or think.

Sit still for a bit and ask God what He wants you to do today—right where you are, even if where you are isn't where you wanted to be. Write His answer in your journal, and then later today, write about what happened when you followed His lead. What did you do? What did you give? Who got a surprise blessing because of you?

DAY 29

HALT

Now all glory to God, who is able, through his mighty power at work within us, to accomplish infinitely more than we might ask or think.

How are you feeling now that you are about to conclude three-fourths of this journey? Journeys can take a hidden toll on us, can't they? That's why another hindrance to our Ephesians 3:20 journey is not taking proper care of ourselves. Our journey may be spiritual, but we need to take care of ourselves physically and mentally as well.

HALT is an acrostic many counselors use as an evaluation tool for the weary. It represents four ways in which we should continuously examine ourselves to stay physically and mentally strong. H stands for hungry, A stands for angry, L for lonely, and T for tired.

I encourage you to evaluate how you are doing today. Use your journal to respond to the following questions.

- *Hungry:* Are you eating well? Is your body being supplied with the nutrients it needs to function at its best?

- *Angry:* How about tension? Are you easily angered? Are you sleeping, exercising, doing what's needed to keep stress levels down and happy hormones up?

· *Lonely:* Are you taking time for those friendships we have talked so much about?

· *Tired:* How tired are you? Are you sleeping? So often things look much different after a good night's rest.

I'm reminded of the old saying: If the devil can't make you bad, he'll make you busy. Don't be fooled into equating busyness with godliness. Before you begin your last ten days of this devotional, stop and allow physical rest for your body while remembering that God's power remains at work to complete within you His "infinitely more." Resting in this truth, you can go above and beyond physical rest and enter into God's spiritual rest.

DAY 30

Bankable Truths

Now all glory to God, who is able, through his mighty power at work within us, to accomplish infinitely more than we might ask or think.

Suppose I handed you a new, crisp $100 bill. Would you immediately think, *Oh my, just imagine what I can do with that!* What if I crumpled it right before your eyes? What if I threw the bill on the ground, stomped on it until it was barely recognizable, and declared its unworthiness to all who could hear? If you're like me, you'd still want it, because no matter what anybody says, a beat-up $100 bill is still worth a hundred dollars.

Now consider what God sees this morning as He looks upon your Ephesians 3:20 journey. He sees that you have been scuffed by life's disappointments and challenges. He sees your struggle with hurtful voices of the past. Yet God beckons you to continue your journey with confidence in His truth. What is the truth? That you are loved. That you are His chosen child. That today holds not just any plan, but *your* plan—and a very worthy and significant plan it is. And a final truth: That absolutely nothing, no one, no circumstance, nor any word from anyone, can devalue you or take from you what God has given.

Just as surely as God has delivered a new day, He delivers new possibilities. Find your quiet place—

in your car as you head off to work, in your kitchen as you plan dinner, or on the walk to your next class. Silence the voices from your past—even those from the past few days. Take just a minute for God; He has a message for you. Be still. Listen. What is that? Do you hear your Creator as He smiles at you and declares: *Oh my, just imagine what I am about to do with you today!* Write a prayer of response in your journal, telling Him how much you look forward to spending your day in His company.

> *"For I know the plans I have for you," declares the LORD, "plans to prosper you and not to harm you, plans to give you hope and a future." (Jeremiah 29:11)*

DAY 31

Seven Simple Words

Now all glory to God, who is able, through his mighty power at work within us, to accomplish infinitely more than we might ask or think.

Peter was a pro; he knew what to do—and he had done it. But though he had fished all night, he hadn't caught a thing. He was exhausted. Empty-handed. Embarrassed. But just as Peter was rolling up his nets and giving up, Jesus came along and said, "Launch out into the deep water."

Can you picture Peter rolling his eyes?

"Go deeper!" Jesus challenged. Jesus believed in Peter and had big plans for him. However, Peter had to think beyond what he, in his strength, could do. He needed to see and know what only God and His power working within him could do.

Have you ever been to a sporting event where the fans called to struggling players: "Dig deep!" What did that mean? What does Christ mean when He tells you to go deeper? He is talking about resolve—not giving up even when all seems lost. He is talking about focus, not on how people are reacting but rather on what God is asking. He is urging you to go beyond your feelings, your talents, and your resources to stand on what you know God has promised, and what only His power at work in you can do. He is talking about looking beyond the obvious to see things yet to be seen—that God is working and, at just the right moment, your obedience will be rewarded "infinitely more" than you could have imagined.

Peter might have rolled his eyes at Jesus' instructions, but his words revealed his willing heart: "But because you say so, I will" (Luke 5:5). Seven simple words.

Is God urging you to go deeper in some area of your life? Describe what you hear Him asking of you. Then, if you are ready to do so, write a prayer to God that echoes Peter's seven simple words. They changed his life. They will change yours as well.

DAY 32

Believe, Act, Receive

Now all glory to God, who is able, through his mighty power at work within us, to accomplish infinitely more than we might ask or think.

You have completed a month of devotionals! How has God grown, changed, challenged, and prepared you? How I wish I could read your journal and discover what His power looks like at work in *your* life!

As we continue this journey together, let's peer into an evening the disciples shared with Jesus.

We're traveling to the shores of the Sea of Galilee to sit among some five thousand men, along with their wives and children. Jesus has just finished speaking, and the sun is beginning to set.

> *Toward evening the disciples approached him. "We're out in the country and it's getting late. Dismiss the people so they can go to the villages and get some supper."*
>
> *But Jesus said, "There is no need to dismiss them. You give them supper."*
>
> *"All we have are five loaves of bread and two fish," they said. Jesus said, "Bring them here." (Matthew 14:15–18 MSG)*

Can you imagine what the disciples thought as Jesus asked for five loaves of bread and two small fish to feed that crowd? Clearly this time Jesus had finally lost His mind!

But whatever the disciples thought, they did not allow their lack of understanding to deter their obedience. Certainly they had questions and doubts, yet the disciples chose to do exactly what Jesus had asked them. And because of their obedience, they became participants in one of the most talked about and beloved miracles of the Bible.

Isn't this what you desire? To be a part of something so much bigger than what you alone can accomplish? If this is your goal, you need to follow the path that the disciples took: "Trust in the Lord with all your heart and lean not on your own understanding; in all your ways submit to him" (Proverbs 3:5–6).

The disciples veered beyond what seemed understandable and trusted Jesus. Next, they did something few would choose: They acted on that trust. Because He said so, they did.

How do you view the "infinitely more" God has challenged you with during this Ephesians 3:20 devotional? Are you overwhelmed? Full of questions? Pause sometime today to reflect on your journey so far. Are you surprised by all that God has been doing? Can you even imagine what else He has in store for you when you choose to move ahead—even when you don't quite understand what He's up to?

DAY 33

None Too Small

Now all glory to God, who is able, through his mighty power at work within us, to accomplish infinitely more than we might ask or think.

What if, at this point in our devotional together, you are feeling underwhelmed? Maybe you are thinking, *Isn't there something more significant and meaningful I can do? What purpose is served by such tiny actions?* Perhaps your notes from earlier devotions include scribbles like "Send a card" or "Call Carol about lunch" or "Share this with Janice."

On Day 24 we talked about the necessity of throwing off things that hinder, but Hebrews 12:1 does not end there. To come through this journey ready to run, we must also throw off "the sin that so easily entangles."

I could insert here a list of "thou shalt nots," but why waste valuable time talking about the obvious transgressions when we can go deeper and talk about the *real* sin that holds us hostage. If not confronted, this sin will rob you of the very life you seek—the life filled with daily invitations to allow God's power to work through you to do infinitely more than you can think or imagine.

This sin that so easily entangles is the sin of believing the lie. In one version, the lie says that what you're being challenged to do is too big, that you can't do it, that your days are too busy and your hurts are too deep. In another version, the lie says that what you're being asked to do is too small and insignificant, that these things don't really matter, that you need not bother because it will make no difference anyway.

What if the disciples from yesterday's devotion had believed either of those lies? The "it's too big" lie would have made them miss out on a miracle. But what about the "it's too small" lie? Walk with me into that crowd for a moment to a small, probably shy lad with a meager lunch. What if, when challenged to give up his meal, he had believed his offering was too small? What if he had declined? Truly, who could have imagined the difference his little loaves of bread and fish were about to make?

Jesus could. Only He knows the difference His power can make to, through, and because of your life.

First Peter 1:13 says to prepare your mind—in other words, "Take charge, people!" It's time to untangle your mind from the size of the task to the real issue: your obedience to the task. God used the little lad's meager offering to feed the multitude. What is it that you have deemed underwhelming that God has an overwhelming purpose for?

DAY 34

The Power to Care

Now all glory to God, who is able, through his mighty power at work within us, to accomplish infinitely more than we might ask or think.

It is not easy to do what you feel God is asking on your best days. But what about on those days when you feel broken by the hurt, disappointment, or sadness of your life? How do you care for others, or do for others, when you can barely care for yourself?

Think back for a moment to Jesus feeding the five thousand. He had already taught them and healed their sick. Then, rather than heeding the disciples' request to send them home to eat, Jesus stayed, performed the miracle, and helped serve the estimated fifteen thousand (counting the wives and children). Matthew 14:20 says Jesus worked until the last person was fed and full.

I can go on and on about the time and energy involved in that miracle and its aftermath, and the commitment it took, but here's what I think you can relate to most: Jesus worked that day from a broken heart. You see, just minutes before the crowd's arrival, Jesus had been told of the violent beheading of His dear friend, John the Baptist. Jesus had come to this location seeking a place of solitude where He could grieve. Yet, as He saw the crowds approaching, Jesus had compassion upon them.

So many women I know show similar compassion in the midst of pain. Some keep singing with a broken heart. Some keep laughing through fearful times. Some keep doing good for others even when their own illnesses demand so much of them.

To those who demonstrate such compassion, God has great things coming. Twelve baskets of food were left over after the multitude was fed. *Left over!* This abundance is what God has in store for those who see others in distress and care for their needs, even with a broken heart.

So keep your head up. Keep looking today for those who need God's compassion. Write in your journal about how God used you today in spite of the burdens you carry (or more likely, *because* of them). Then give Him thanks for His promise that your time of abundance is coming. Your reward is on its way.

DAY 35

Spelling Lesson

*Now all glory to God, who is able, through his mighty
power at work within us, to accomplish infinitely
more than we might ask or think.*

A granddad overheard something he didn't quite
understand from his granddaughter as she worked
among their flowerbeds. She was repeating the
alphabet as if saying a prayer. Gently approaching
her, he asked, "Whatcha doing?" The little girl looked

up and answered, "I'm praying, but I can't think of exactly the right words. So I'm just saying all the letters. God will put them together for me, because He knows all the right words."

I love this story for so many reasons, but topping that list would be the reminder of the trust and rest we can have each time we pray. When we don't know the perfect words, we can depend on God's perfect will.

As you choose the trust that brings God's peace today, you will be comforted. But not only that, your life will spell out the powerful message of Jesus' words in John 14:1: "Do not let your hearts be troubled. You believe in God; believe also in me."

When you don't know what to think or say, continue praying and trusting in the One who knows. Let Him arrange the alphabet of your prayers. And if you'd like to have a little fun in your journal today, list the letters of the alphabet down the left side of the page. Then next to those letters, write a word or phrase about God that starts with that letter. For example, A: Awesome, B: Beautiful, C: Caring, and so on.

We do not know what we ought to pray for, but the Spirit himself intercedes for us through wordless groans. (Romans 8:26)

DAY 36

Calm Inside and Out

Now all glory to God, who is able, through his mighty power at work within us, to accomplish infinitely more than we might ask or think.

When circumstances, choices, or other's devices seem to be against you, cling to this powerful call-to-action promise: "If you remain in me and my words remain in you, ask whatever you wish, and it will be done for you" (John 15:7). In doing your part, you have God's promise He will do His. So rather than allowing any circumstance to have power over you, you can take back your life.

Abundant life is not achieved by doing what comes naturally. It is achieved by choosing to do what comes unnaturally! You choose to do what is right even when it is not what you would like. Rather than becoming angry, resentful, revengeful, or defeated, you choose to stop and pray. You regroup and ask God what His word is on the matter. Then, to "remain" in that word, you look for opportunities to do the right thing, no matter how fearful or intimidating, how unnatural or uncomfortable.

Whenever I teach this principle I think of my youngest son, Austin, and one of his baseball games. He was five or six years old and was playing first base (not his regular position) when the opposing team's batter hit a pop-up. The ball looked as if it was going to the moon before beginning its descent. With two outs, Austin needed this catch to secure the win. He stood calmly, glove poised, and made the catch!

After the game, reluctant to profess how unnerved I'd been by the play, I decided to applaud him for his coolness and confidence in a difficult situation. "Wow, Austin," I began, "what a great job you did! I would have been scared, but you were so calm out there!" Looking up at me, his eyes revealed the struggle he had overcome. "I may have been calm on the outside, Mommy, but I was shaking on the inside!"

From my little boy's confession came a deep biblical principle that will forever inspire me. Today, I hope it also inspires you and reminds you that even as life pushes you beyond your comfort zone, you can choose to do what seems unnatural but right. You can confront what is being thrown at you with God's word along with your glove of determination, faith, perseverance, and trust. By standing, confronting, and doing, you begin achieving with calmness and confidence what God has promised: the "infinitely more" that is to come in your life.

What "fly ball" is being thrown at you today? Write a prayer to God, asking Him to remind you of His great promises and unchanging character whenever you start to wobble.

DAY 37

Believing the Best

Now all glory to God, who is able, through his mighty power at work within us, to accomplish infinitely more than we might ask or think.

A little boy went out to the backyard to play with a baseball and bat. He said to himself, "I am the best hitter in the world." Then he threw the ball up in the air, took a swing at it, and missed. Without a moment's hesitation, he tossed it in the air again, saying as he swung the bat, "I'm the best hitter in the world." Again, he missed. Strike two. He tossed the ball a third time, even more determined, saying, "I am the best hitter in the world!" But he missed again. Strike three. The boy set down his bat with the biggest smile ever. "Well, what do you know," he said, "I'm the best *pitcher* in the world!"

Proverbs 23:7 says as we think, we become. What we believe, we receive. Take whatever comes your way today, and rather than expecting the same old, same old, take charge by expecting more. Then make your actions match your expectations. Do what a winner would do. Begin living as if the "infinitely more" has already happened. Then tell your journal what happened!

DAY 38

Be Available

Now all glory to God, who is able, through his mighty power at work within us, to accomplish infinitely more than we might ask or think.

You've almost made it to the end of this journey together. Perhaps you're now wondering, *How can I keep on experiencing the daily "more" that God has planned for me?*

This is how: by rolling up your sleeves and doing what you can do, knowing that it is God's power within you that will complete the "more." Sound easy? Well, not really. But manageable? Yes. And worth it? Absolutely!

While writing about my own Ephesians 3:20 journey, I had to be faithful to do what was Kim-possible with full expectation that God would come through with the impossible. You see, I can stand before any crowd and speak comfortably because I let my audience guide me to what needs to be said. I watch their faces, their posture. Somehow, I sense God showing me if I'm being too harsh, too tentative, and so on. But when writing, I can't see faces. I don't know when my words need to be softened or when I need to issue a stronger challenge. When God called me to the "more" of writing, it was a much bigger "more" than what I knew I could do. So, I asked God what He expected of me. He said, *Be available*.

To make myself available, I first committed my mind to the challenge. Then I placed my confidence in the promise of His power working through me. Next, I had to discipline myself so I could stay prepared for His power to flow. This required commitment to the little stuff: rolling out of bed by 4:30 every morning— at home or away; taking vitamins and eating healthy to ensure energy; running each morning; declining invitations that would keep me up too late. But as I was faithful in doing what little I could do, God was even more faithful in completing what He had promised to do.

You have that same promise of God's faithfulness today. As you face the impossibility of your "more"—restoring that friendship, saving that marriage, beginning that Bible study at school, starting an exercise program, daring to reveal your secret—identify what you *can* do. And when it is time, take that next step. Don't let anyone tell you that you can't. Remain confident of this: that He who begins a good work promises to carry it on to its completion (see Philippians 1:6).

What good work is God asking you to do? What changes in your mindset, schedule, or lifestyle can you make to become more ready and available? If you're ready to act, He's ready too!

DAY 39

Messes Welcome

Now all glory to God, who is able, through his mighty
power at work within us, to accomplish infinitely
more than we might ask or think.

It was 1990. Lee and I were preparing for his parents'
visit. Minutes before their arrival, Lee had freshened
the outside plants with another dousing of water
and after days of cleaning, I had finally gotten things
perfect inside. Telling our toddler, Trey, to sit tight, I

ran upstairs for a last bit of make-up. Within minutes I heard unfamiliar sounds. *Swoosh. Thud. Swoosh. Thud.* What in the world? *Swooooosh. Thud!* Rounding the corner, I looked down to see the biggest smile ever on Trey's little face. He pulled his surprise from "behind" his back (it was so large it didn't really fit behind his back).

"Look Mommy, I brought you a flower!" Trey had tried to pick a day lily. Instead, I guess because it had been newly watered, the entire plant popped right out. The swoosh was the mud being dragged through the house, and the thud was the sound made each time the plant hit another of the white carpeted steps.

I guess a lot of things could have gone through my mind, but looking into those sweet eyes my thoughts were overwhelmed by such a loving heart and grand gesture, all to make his mommy smile.

Dear friend, if you are wondering and worrying this morning if the challenge before you *is* really from God, then worry no longer. Just do it! Don't be afraid of disappointing God, falling flat on your face, or completely messing up trying to please God. Consider my heart toward my toddler, and then imagine the heart of God as He looks upon you this morning. He could never be disappointed as you strive to please Him. He looks way beyond the works of your hands to the love in your heart. And your Heavenly Father pauses today and says, *Well done! Well done, my good and faithful child.*

Are you worried about disappointing God today? Write a descriptive word or phrase in your journal to describe your worry. Then draw a slash through that word, and draw a heart around it. Think of your fear as being wrapped in God's love. Then move into your day with the confidence of a dearly loved child.

DAY 40

A Banquet Ahead

Now all glory to God, who is able, through his mighty power at work within us, to accomplish infinitely more than we might ask or think.

Welcome to the last day of your Ephesians 3:20 journey! Do you remember how your journey began? It was with a little girl who loved her imitation pearls.

What imitation pearls did you discover you were holding on to ever so tightly? Have you come to realize that what you hold on to—yesterday's dreams, unfulfilled wishes, abandoned relationships—has left you feeling empty? You understand perhaps, as I do now, that what you have tucked away is tarnished. No wonder you keep it hidden, afraid to let anyone see or know how damaged it really is. Those things you grasp for comfort—lifestyles, habits, addictions— hold hostage the life God wants you to experience.

So here's the real challenge: What are you going to do about it now? Are you willing to offer all that you are and all that you have been through in exchange for God's greater offer to work in your life? To accomplish infinitely and abundantly more than you could ever imagine? How will you respond to this forty-day journey you've taken?

I'll go first and tell you how I ended these forty days—with a renewed commitment to do what God asks of me in sharing this message of hope: *Glory to God, who is able, through his mighty power at work within us, to accomplish infinitely more than we might ask or think.* I will travel, write, and share my "pearls"—my life and each incident—with as much vulnerability and transparency as God asks. My hope is that those with whom I share will be awakened to the importance of sharing their stories as well. From this moment forward, I pray, because of God's power at work within me, that God will allow me to encourage every woman I encounter to dare to believe He not only can but also yearns to use every pearl, tarnished or real, from her past as a tool of ministry and hope for her future. My greatest desire is for each of us to emerge from behind our masks to show our true selves. Our fearfully and wonderfully made selves. The selves God loved so much that He gave His only begotten Son so that we may not only have life, but abundant life. Not because of who we are, but because of who Jesus is and because of His mighty power at work within us.

My message is, and always will be, the same: No matter what burdens you bear from your past or your present, God has the power to turn those burdens into blessings. When you offer them to Him, you will fulfill your life in such a way that your blessings will overflow and become God's blessings of encouragement and inspiration to all those people around you. Dare to believe!

Thank you for going on this forty-day journey with me. Keep pressing on! I hope you know this is only the appetizer. A lifelong banquet awaits as you continue to respond to and act upon the truths God has shown you. I would be honored to hear from you about how your life is being transformed.

About the Author

Kim Crabill is the founder and director of Roses and Rainbows Ministries, Inc. She is the author of seven books and booklets, including her signature work, *Burdens to Blessings: Discovering the Power of Your Story.* Her message and materials reach an international audience through conferences and retreats, adult and high school curriculum, prison educational programs, and military transitional support.

Kim serves on the advisory board of the Christian Women in Media Association (CWIMA). She was named "Outstanding Leader in Media" for 2017 to

2018 by the CWIMA and was featured in London's *Highly Fabulous* magazine by Dr. Patricia Benjamin as a "2018 International Woman of Influence." She hosts the television show *Burdens to Blessings with Kim Crabill* on NRBTV and is also the host of the morning radio talk show *COFFEE with Kim*.

Kim travels globally to inspire audiences to discover the power of their own stories.